AF486750

YOU
NEED
You

YOU NEED You

A Name God Calls Himself-

God's Love for Children & Teens

By Jordan Countee

Inspired by the Holy Spirit

YOU NEED YOU
You Need You © 2025 Jordan Countee

All rights reserved. This book or parts thereof may not be reproduced in any form, stored in a retrieval system, or transmitted in any form by any means – electronic, mechanical, photocopy, recording, or otherwise – without prior written permission of the publisher, except as provided by the United States of America copyright law.

ISBN: 979-8-9925856-8-1

Quill and Company Publishing

QuillandCompany.com
TheQuillandCompany@gmail.com

*In loving memory of Uncle Timmy
and Jerome "Popop" Countee*

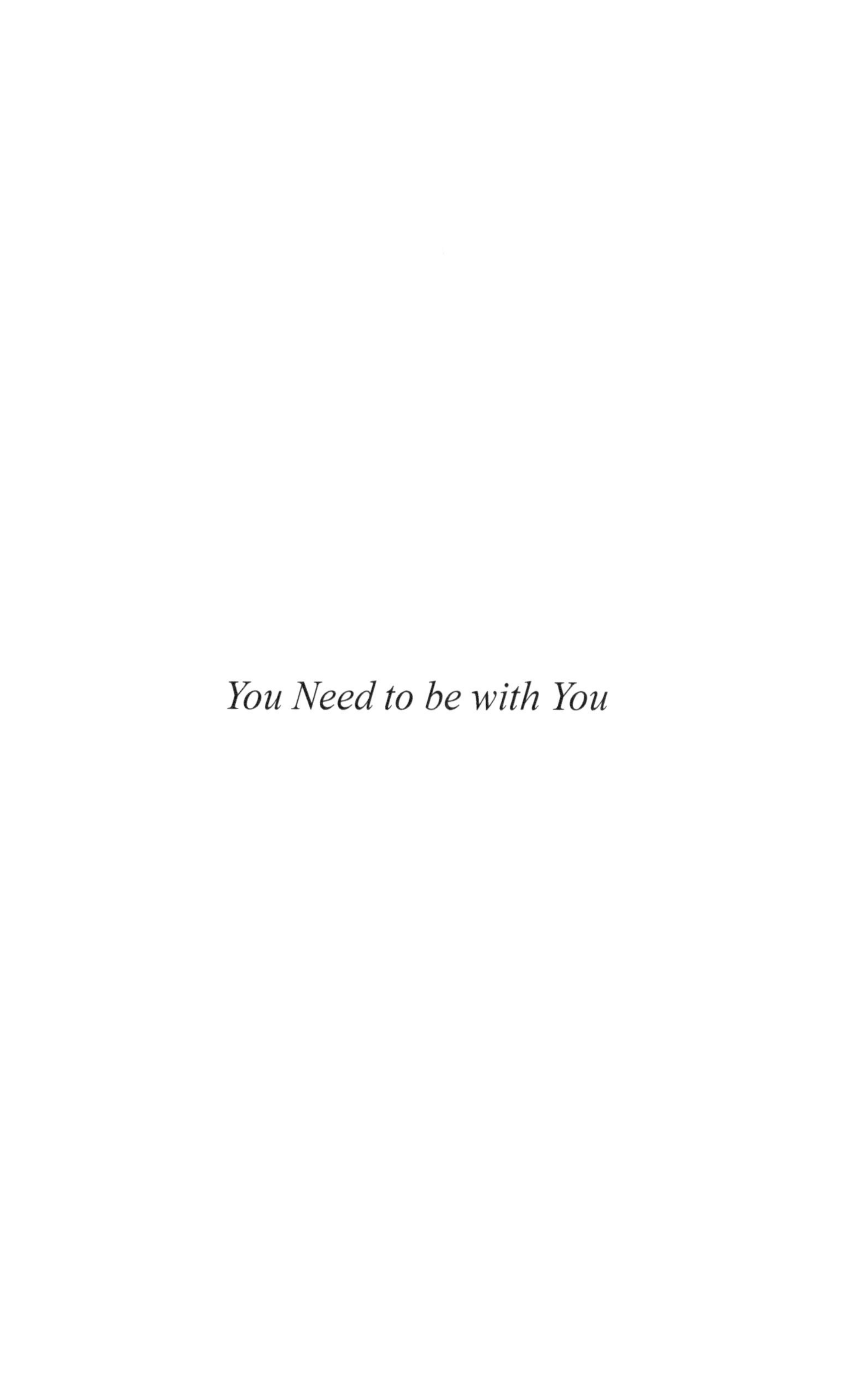

You Need to be with You

What is a Prayer?

A prayer is a meaningful conversation with God. You can pray at any time. You can pray anywhere. You can pray for anything. There is nothing He does not know. When you pray to You, remember to remind him that you love, want, and need Him. He prays for you without stopping so never stop praying and believing in Him.

Dear God,

I need You. I need the One who never leaves me.

You need You.

I need You. When I need You, I know I love You. I only want to be for You. Thank You, and I love You.

In Jesus' name, amen.

This is a prayer the Holy Spirit blessed me with. If you do not know God yet, this book will help you meet Him. Ask to be filled with the Holy Spirit.

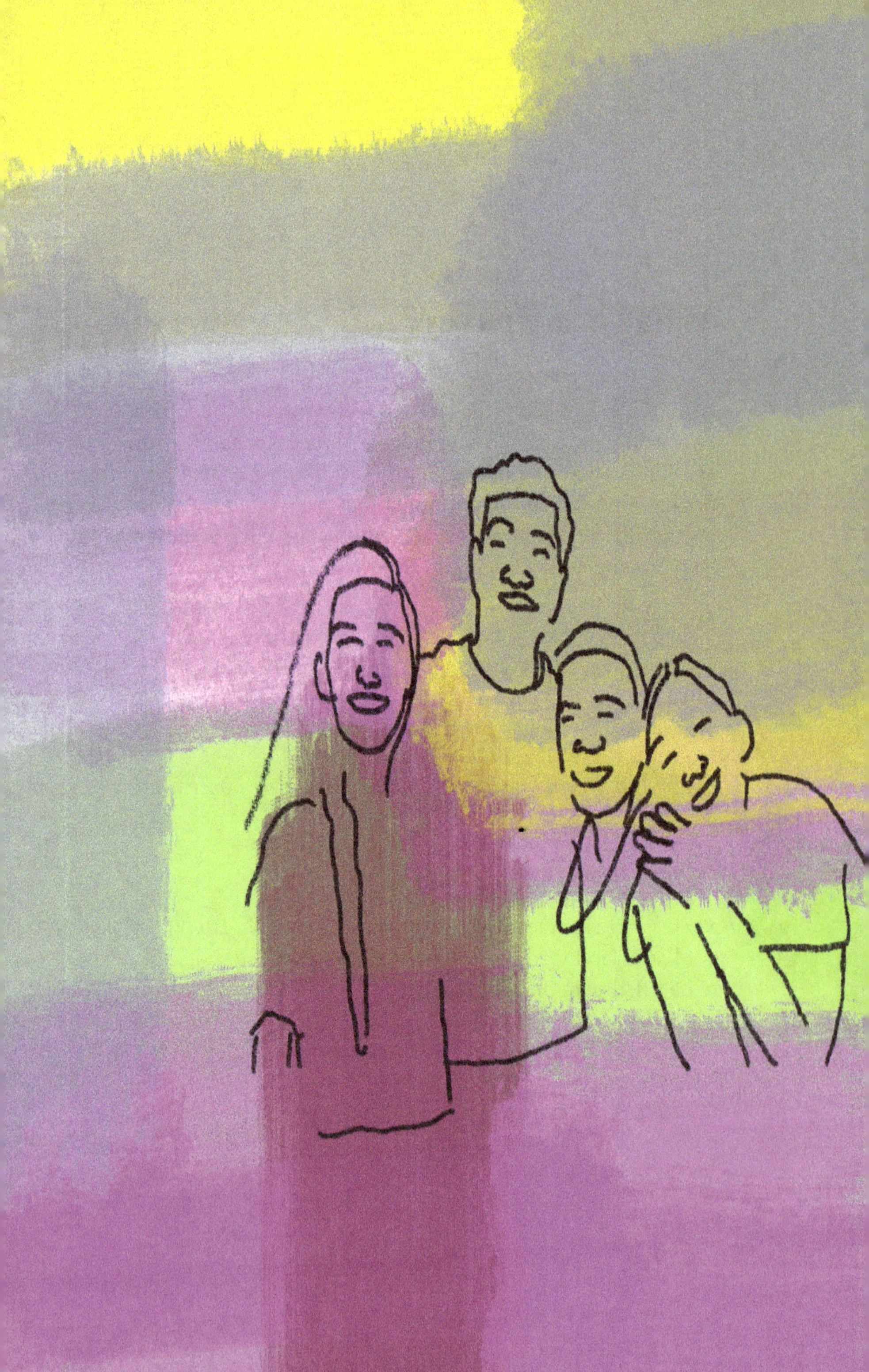

God Needs You

My prayer life grows deeper when I realize how much I need God. He loves me, and I am in love with the way He loves me. But here's something beautiful: **He needs me.** He wants me.

Does He love us all the same? Yes, He does.

This changes everything—the way I see people, the way I understand love. God tells me what to pray for, and suddenly I understand that if I allow Him to show me what to do each day, I can do anything!

The Most High King calls Himself many names. You is one of them. In this book, we'll learn more about this, and meet important people from the bible.

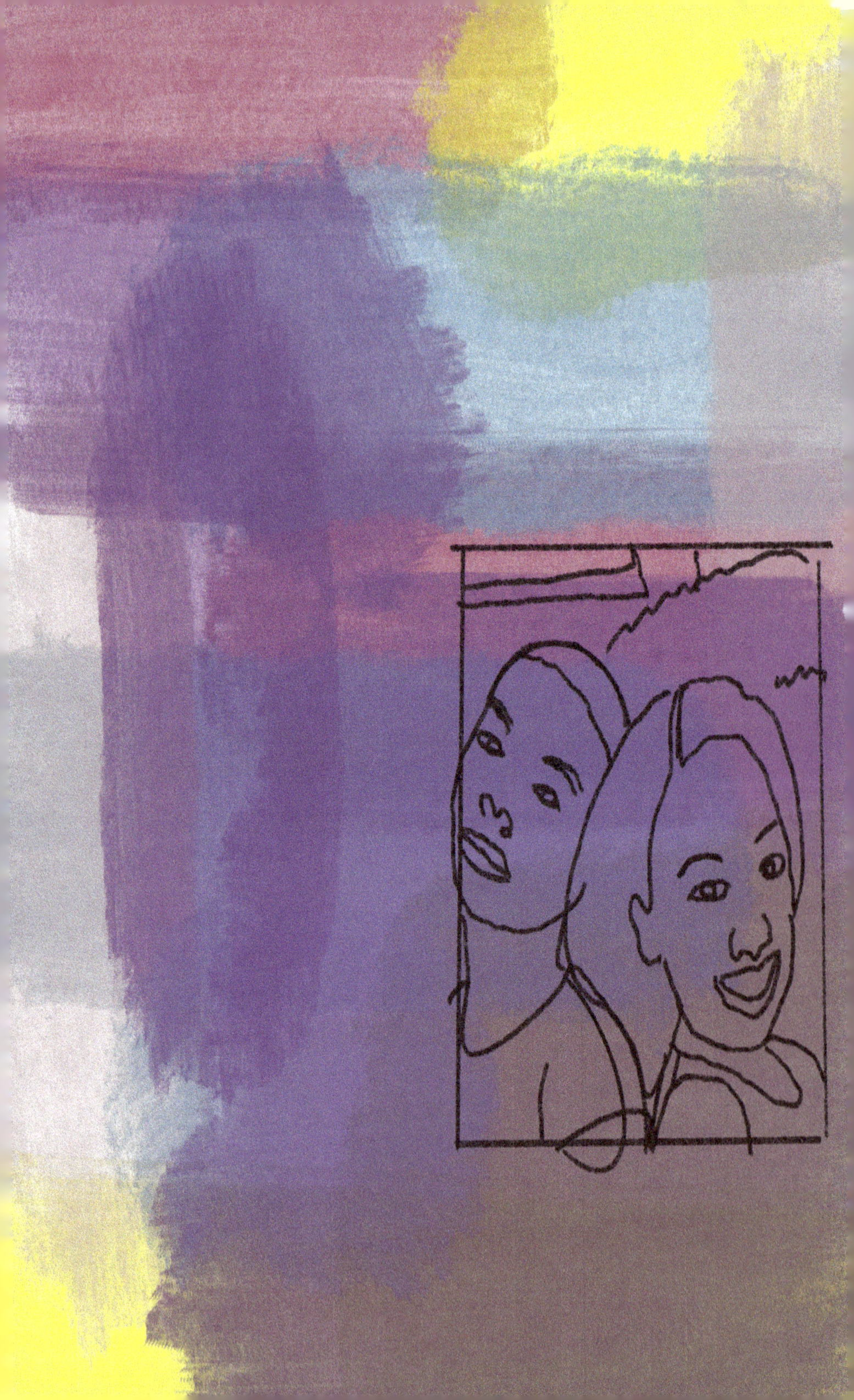

Choosing Wisely

Not everyone we meet will help us grow closer to God. Here are qualities of a person to stay away from:

- People who lie
- People who steal
- People who hurt and abuse others
- Selfish people
- People with sinful habits

It is ok to stay away in order to protect your heart.

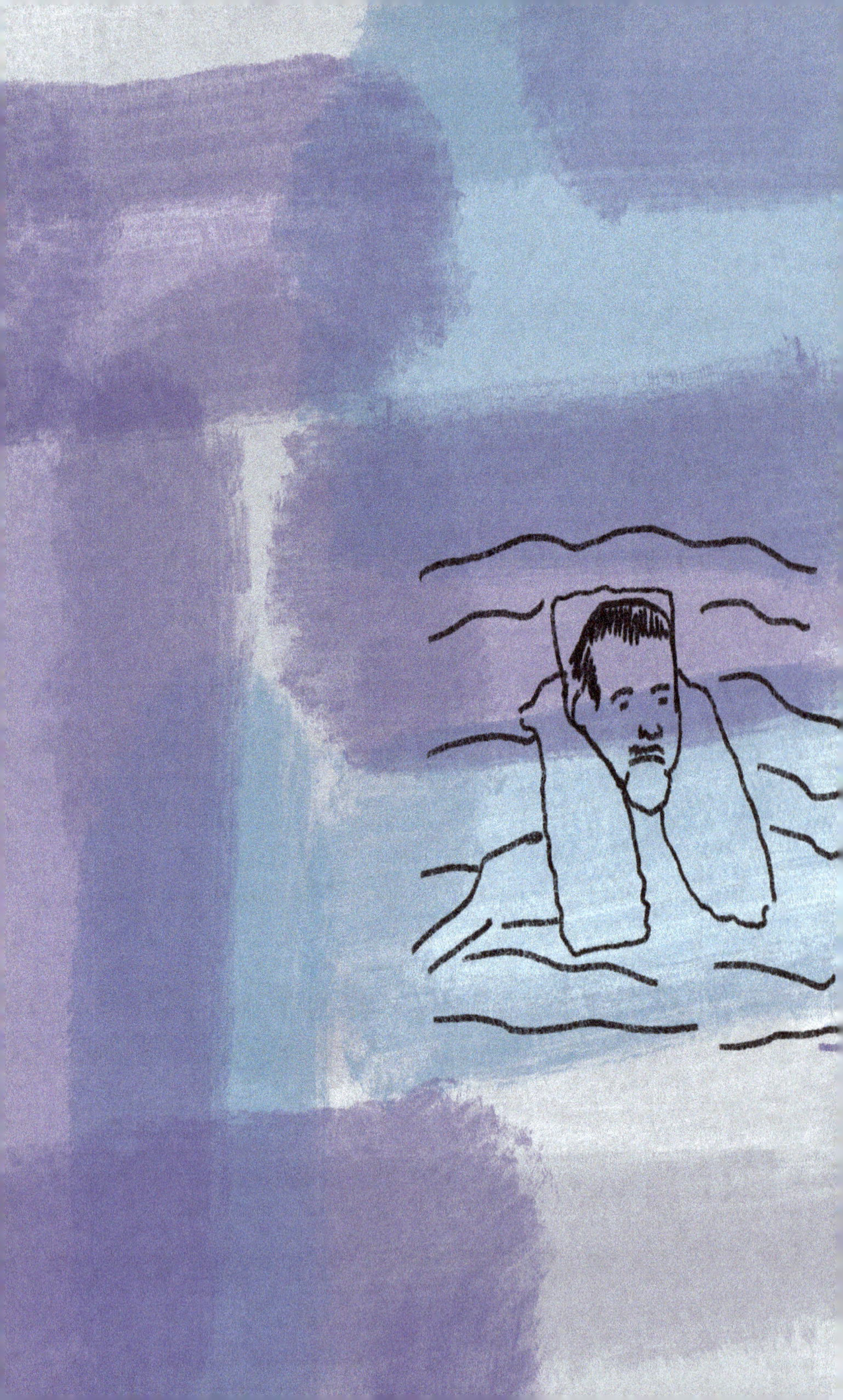

Forgiveness is a Life Jacket

If God can forgive the mess made by every single person, so can you. How did He do it? John 3:16 tells us: **with His love.**

Forgiveness. Pass it on.

Sin is messy. Every sin makes a mess. But we each have access to perfect love and perfect forgiveness.

"Mercy, peace, and love be multiplied to you." — Jude 1:2 (NKJV)

Multiplied means to become greater. When you multiply it grows beyond what it was before." Jude greets us with God's promise that a little mercy, peace, and love will become abundant mercy, peace, and love.

- **Mercy** means someone who could punish you forgives you.
- **Peace** is everything He gives. It is the safety and stillness God gives when you ask for it.
- **Love** happens when someone cares deeply about you

God shows mercy. God is love. God brings peace.

When you show forgiveness, it multiplies. It's a beautiful way to live—an experience that teaches mercy and love. The peace it brings to your life is a blessing.

Let it go. Let the messiness of sin go.

Did you know that nothing can separate you from the love of God? This means **God never leaves you.** He is always with you. He is everywhere.

We show God we love Him when we forgive people. He wants you. He is love.

Peace be still. You are safe and sound.

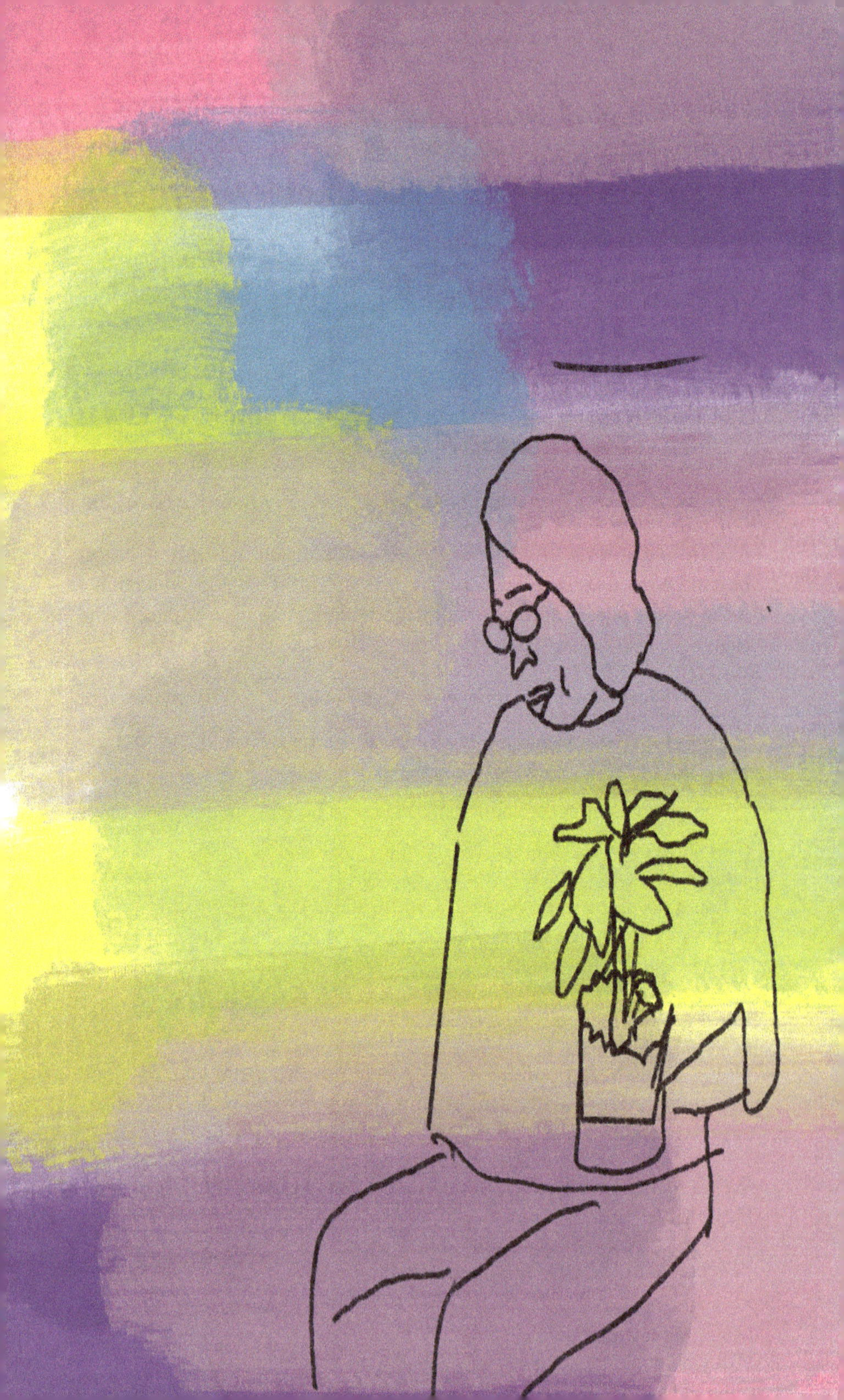

Every Day We Want You

We want You. Every day. In every way. All we do is love you. All we want is You more than anything.

Forgiveness is both an act and a decision to release the pain and ugliness of a sin that hurt you. This allows you to experience a unique kind of freedom.

Imagine you're in the middle of the ocean. If you have a life jacket, you can float.

Now imagine that **forgiveness is that life jacket.**

Even if someone tries to push you down, you cannot sink. Your life jacket gives you the freedom and safety to float and survive. The offense can be forgiven when you talk it out, solve the problem, and swim together to the safety of shore.

Jesus' Family

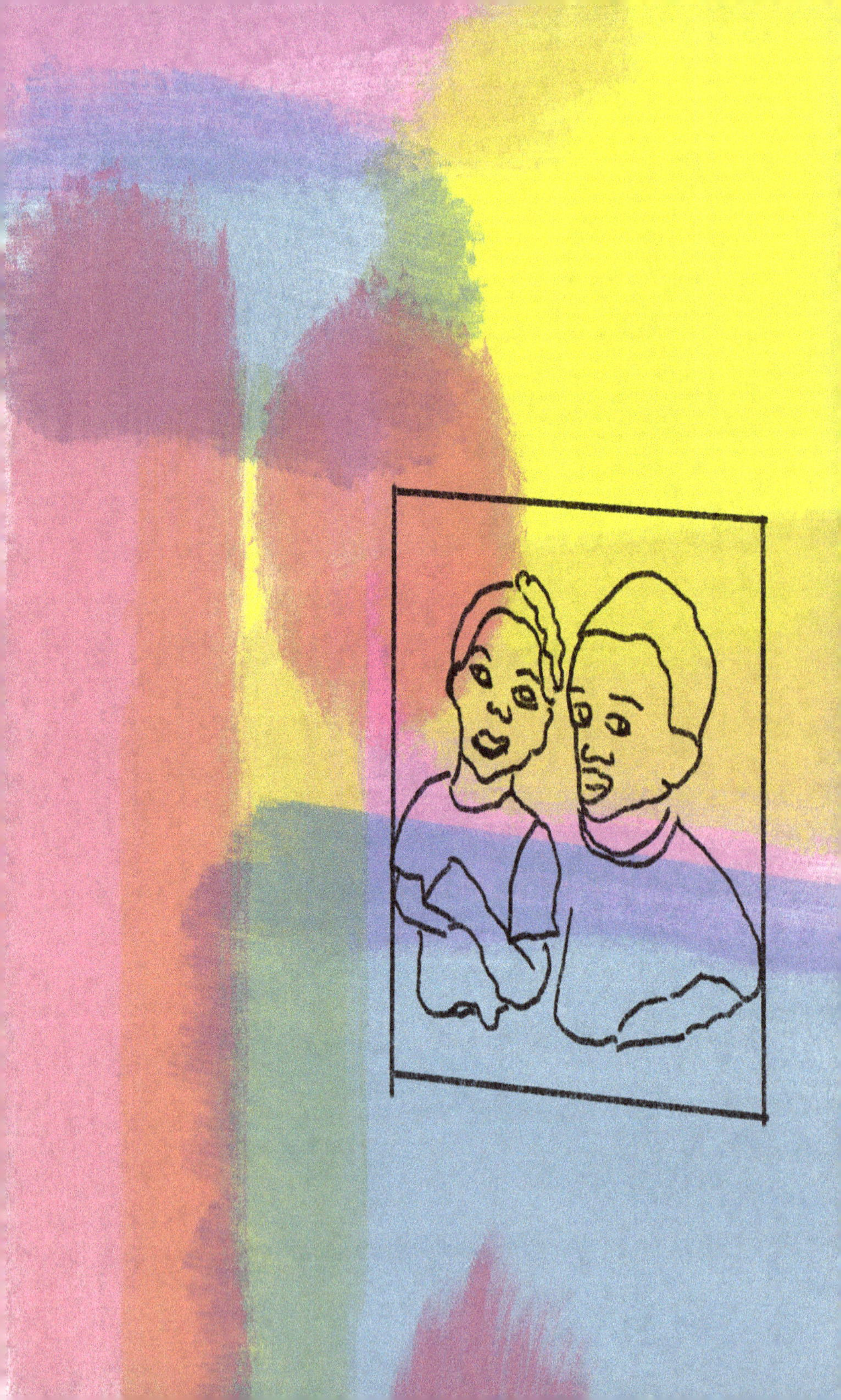

Meet Dad

Meet God the Father. Meet the Holy Spirit.

The Holy Spirit wants to love you.

He is perfect. He is love. He cries tears of joy and sadness. He comes to us like a rushing wind, and He is also the light. He is like fire. The Lion and the Lamb. He is the Most High King, and He is God.

God has an unlimited number of names.

His love story is this:

"For God so loved the world that He gave His only begotten Son, that whoever believes in Him should not perish but have everlasting life."
— John 3:16

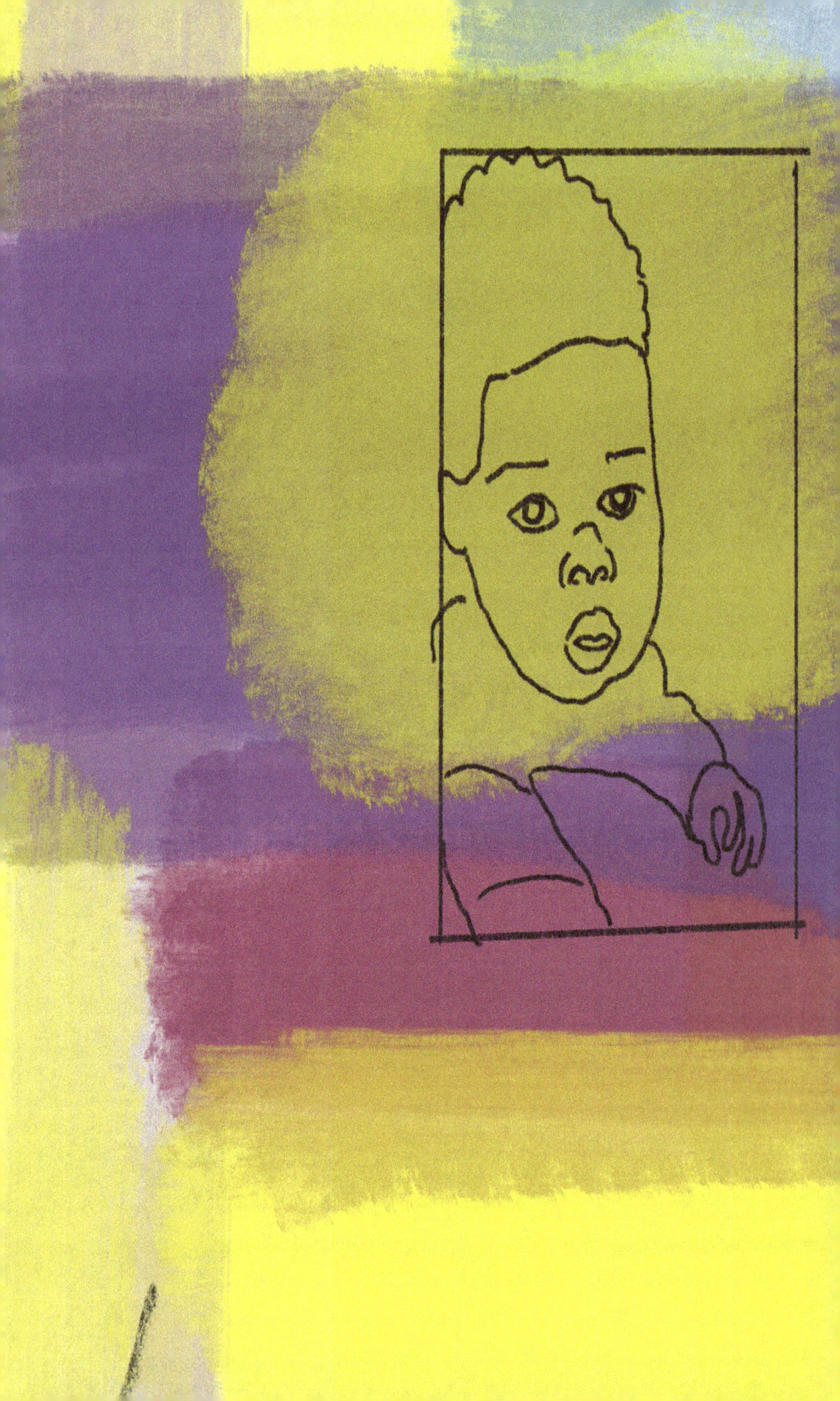

Meet Jesus

Jesus is perfect and never fails. He never leaves us nor forsakes us.

How can we meet God, Jesus, and the Holy Spirit?

Encounter means meeting. To have an encounter, simply speak Jesus' name anywhere, especially in a place of worship. This can be a church or any location where you feel close to God. Listen closely for an introduction or response.

Encounters are wonderful and perfect.

Jesus, we need You. You are the Savior of the world.

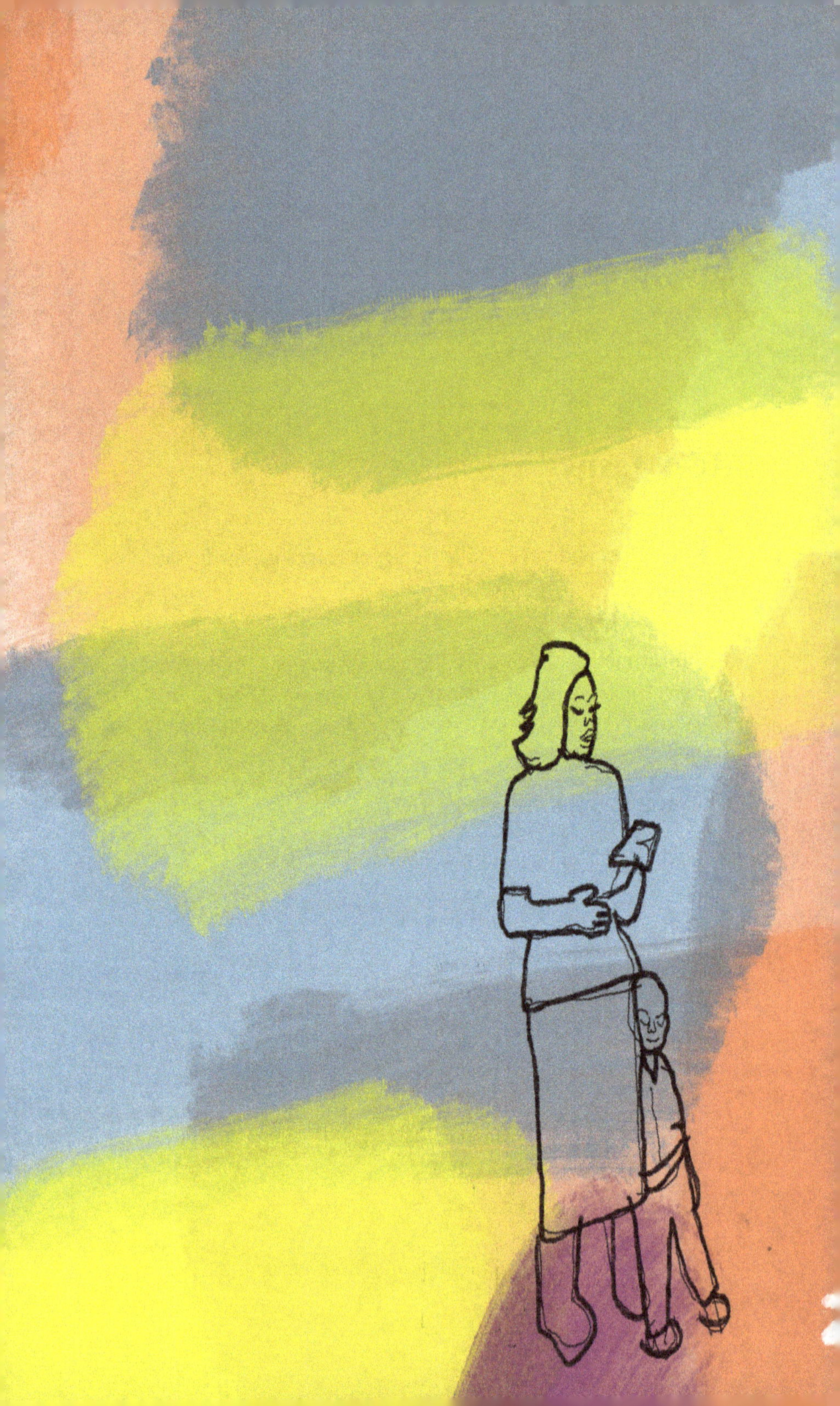

Meet Mom

Mary is blessed. She is full of grace. Mary gave birth to Jesus, who is called the Messiah.

"Now the birth of Jesus Christ was as follows: After His mother Mary was betrothed to Joseph, before they came together, she was found with child of the Holy Spirit." (Matthew 1:18 (NKJV))

To be pregnant means to be with child—Mary was having a baby. The timing was essential to successfully giving birth to the Savior.

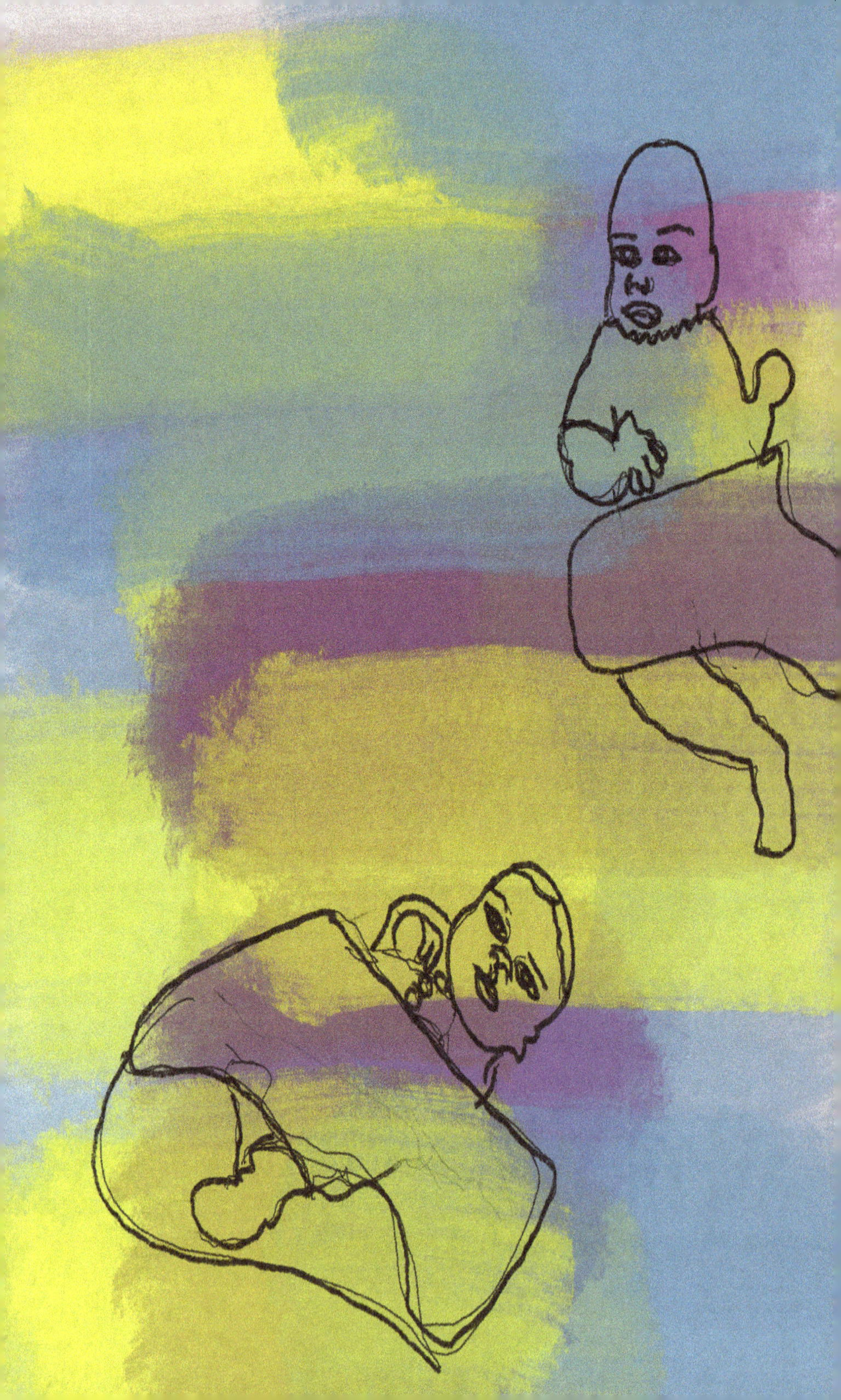

Meet John the Baptist

John the Baptist was born before Jesus. His mother's name was Elizabeth. He is Jesus' cousin.

Jesus, son of Mary, and John, son of Elizabeth, changed the world with their love for God and their love for each other.

While both were still in their mothers' wombs, John leaped for joy when Mary came near because he was excited about Jesus—even before they were born!

Jesus loved John completely. John represents all of us. He taught about the coming of the Messiah. He was pure in heart, and his lifestyle reflected that purity.

God loved both Jesus and John. John spent his entire life sharing his testimony as a witness to the light of the world—Jesus, the Lamb of God, the Lion of Judah, the Rose of Sharon.

In John 1:14, it says that Jesus is the Word who became flesh and lived among us.

John the Baptist baptized people in the river. He loved Jesus so much that he followed Him and taught His teachings. My favorite moment between these cousins was when John baptized Jesus in the Jordan River. **We know we need baptism because Jesus was baptized.**

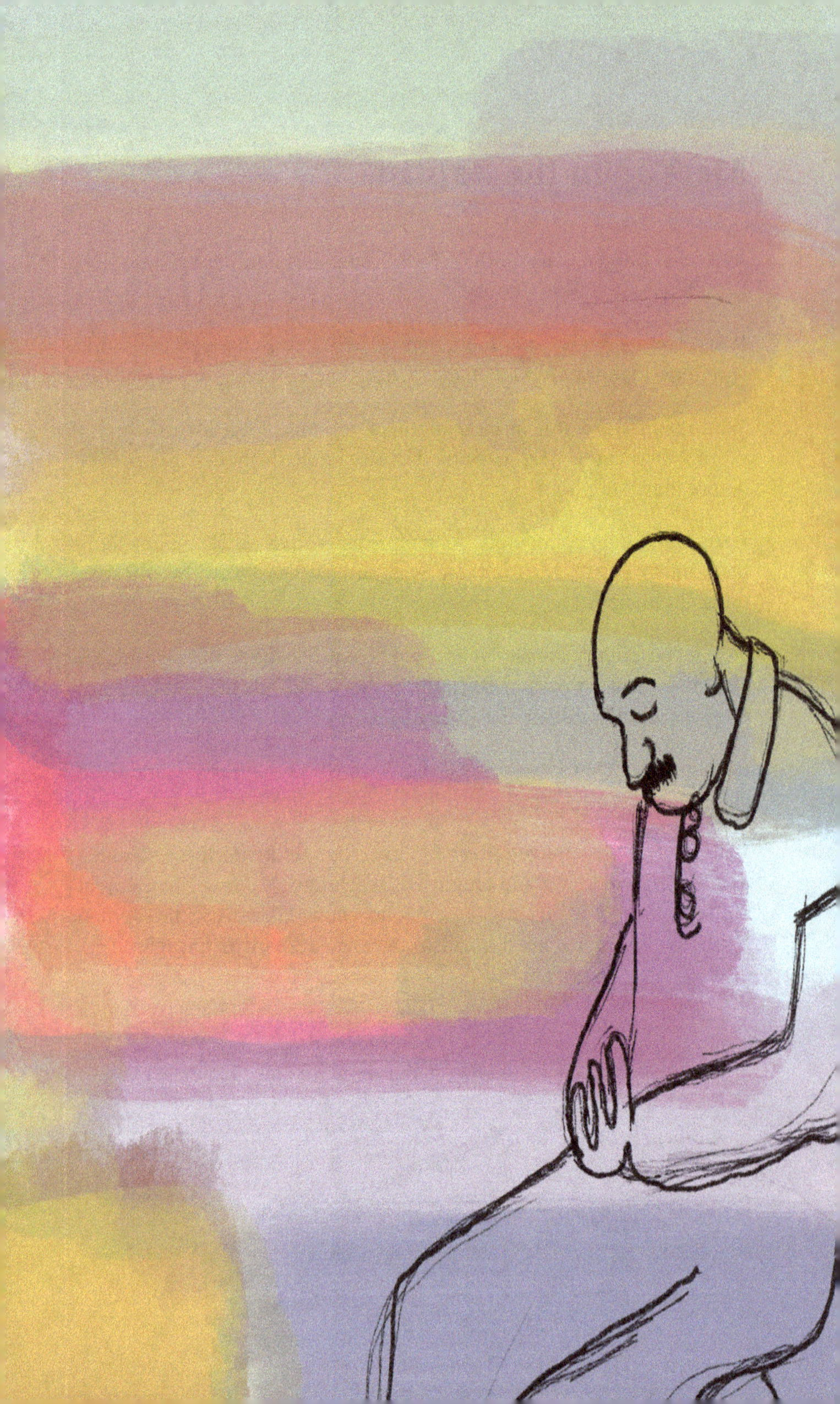

Meet Joseph

Joseph was Mary's "Me". Joseph was engaged to Mary when she became pregnant with Jesus. **Engaged** means they had agreed to get married and start a family.

Joseph was a righteous man. When he discovered Mary was pregnant, he didn't want to disgrace her publicly, so he decided to quietly break their engagement.

But as he thought about this, an angel of the Lord appeared to him in a dream:

"Joseph, son of David, do not be afraid to take Mary as your wife. The child within her was conceived by the Holy Spirit. She will have a son, and you are to name Him Jesus, for He will save His people from their sins." (Matthew 1:20-21 (NKJV))

This fulfilled what the prophet said:

"Look! The virgin will conceive a child! She will give birth to a son, and they will call Him Immanuel, which means 'God is with us.'" (Isaiah 7:14 (NKJV))

When Joseph woke up, he did as the angel commanded and took Mary as his wife. But he did not have relations with her until Jesus was born. And Joseph named Him Jesus.

Joseph obediently led Mary as they traveled to find a safe place where she could give birth to Jesus.

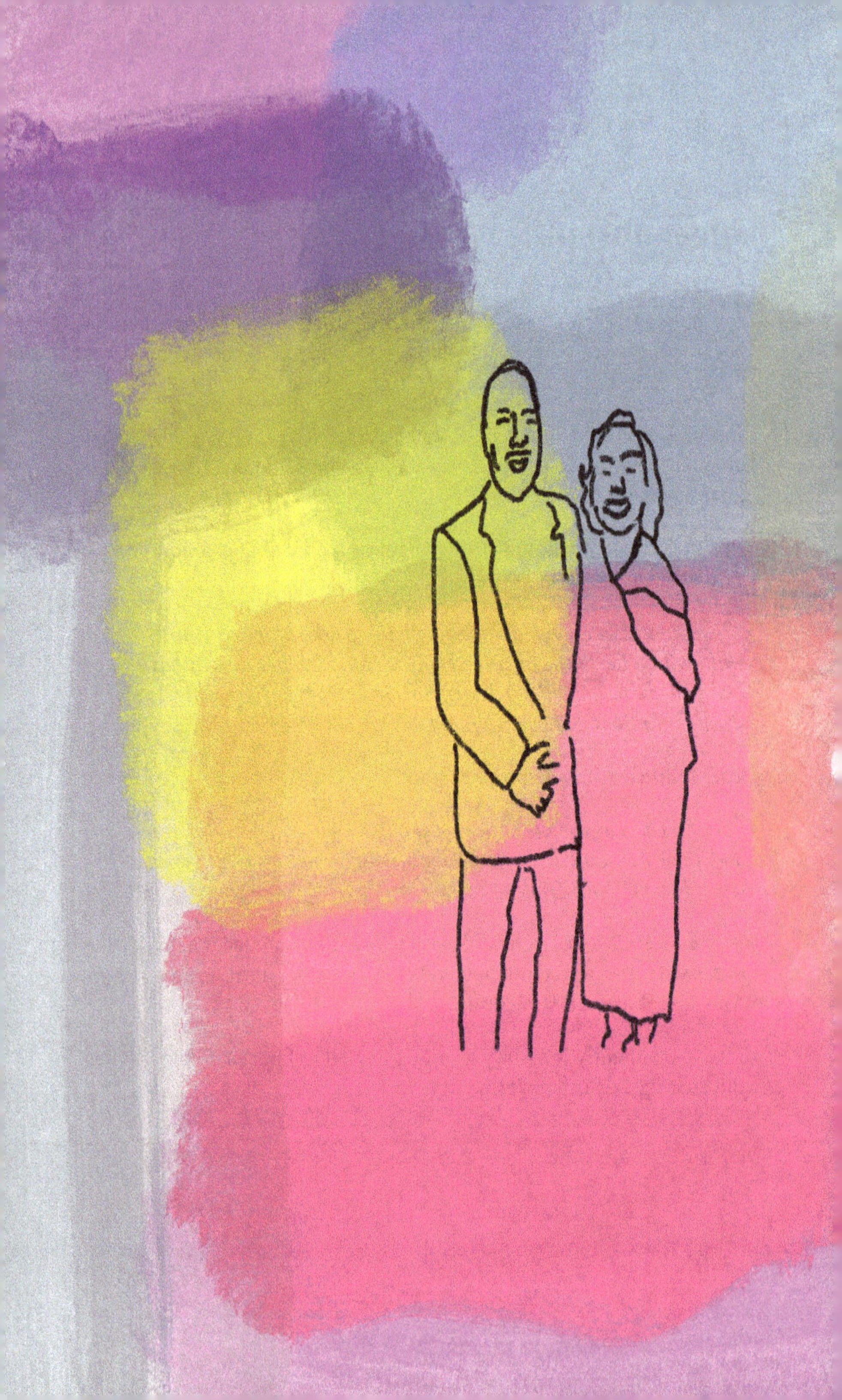

Meet Jude

Jude was a prophet—someone who foresees the will of God. Jude was the half-brother of Jesus of Nazareth.

He wrote the book of Jude, which is an **epistle**—a holy letter in the Bible. His words teach us about mercy, love, and staying close to God.

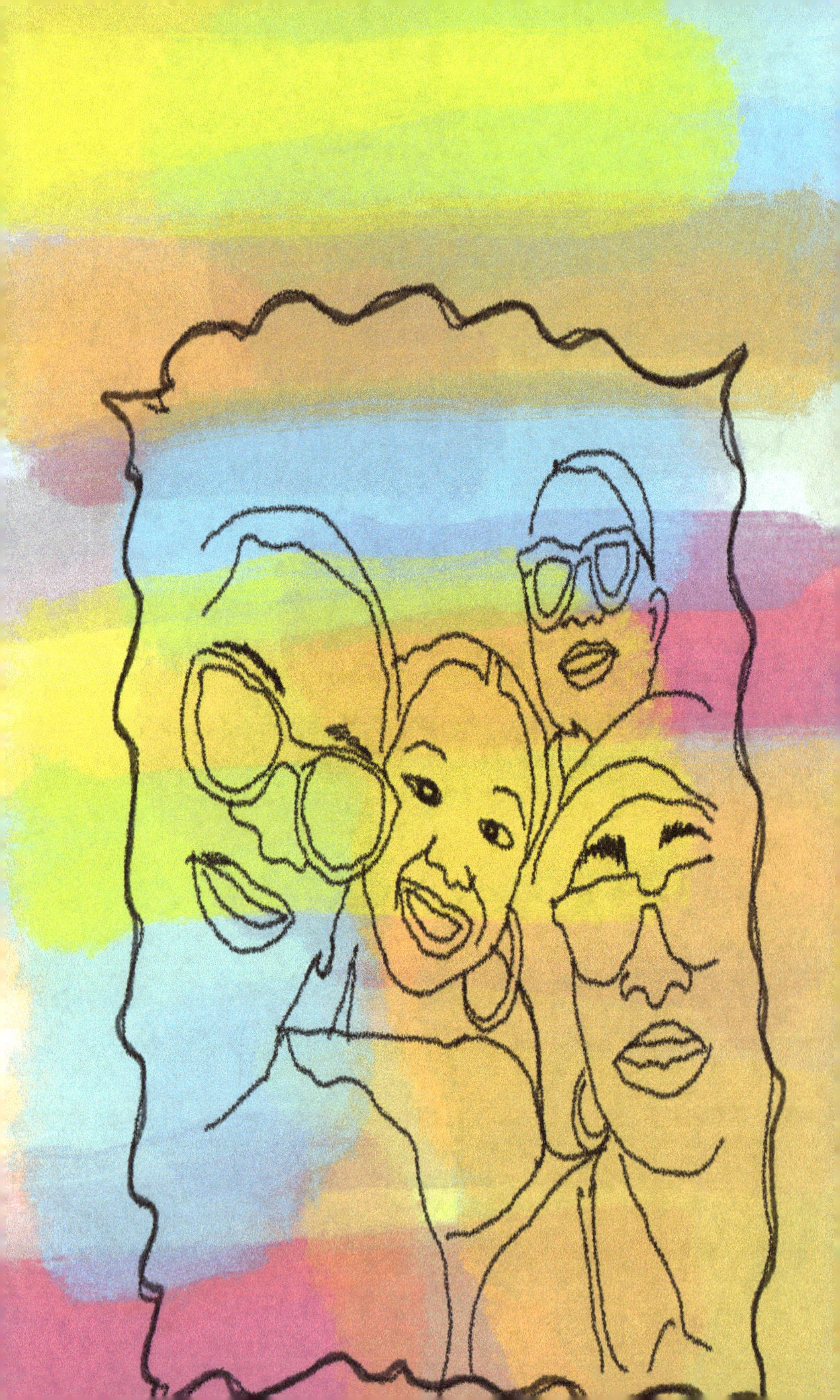

The Journey Begins

Now you've met Them. God the Father, Jesus the Son, the Holy Spirit, and the faithful people who walked with God.

They are waiting to meet you too. All you have to do is call Their names and open your heart.

God never leaves. He is always there. And He loves you more than you could ever imagine.

www.ingramcontent.com/pod-product-compliance
Lightning Source LLC
Chambersburg PA
CBHW071259130726
47998CB00003B/1262